The Antarctic Treaty

Julie Haydon

Australia • Brazil • Japan • Korea • Mexico • Singapore • Spain • United Kingdom • United States

The Antarctic Treaty

Fast Forward
Silver Level 24

Text: Julie Haydon
Editor: Cameron Macintosh
Design: Stella Vassiliou
Series design: James Lowe
Production controller: Seona Galbally
Photo research: Michelle Cottrill
Audio recordings: Juliet Hill, Picture Start
Spoken by: Matthew King and Abbe Holmes

Acknowledgements
The author and publisher would like to acknowledge permission to reproduce material from the following sources: Photographs by Auscape/ Still Pictures, p 21; The Art Archive/ Global Book Publishing, p 6; British Antarctic Survey/ Chris Gilbert, p 13; Corbis/ Kit Kittle, p 18; Getty Images/ AFP, front cover bottom, pp 1 bottom, 17/ Kim Heacox, p 4; National Library of Australia, p 7; Newspix/ KH Mackenzie, p 9/ Mawson Institute, p 8; Photolibrary/ Chris Sattlberger, p 19/ BAS, back cover, p 14/ Doug Allan, p 20/ Geoff Renner, p 22/ Photo Researchers, p 23/ Rick Price, front cover top, pp 1 top, 16/ SPL, p 5.

ISBN 978 0 17 012712 7
ISBN 978 0 17 012705 9 (set)

Cengage Learning Australia
Level 7, 80 Dorcas Street
South Melbourne, Victoria Australia 3205
Phone: 1300 790 853

Cengage Learning New Zealand
Unit 4B Rosedale Office Park
331 Rosedale Road, Albany, North Shore NZ 0632
Phone: 0800 449 725

For learning solutions, visit **cengage.com.au**

Printed in Australia by Ligare Pty Ltd
9 10 11 12 13 14 15 20 19 18 17 16

THE UNIVERSITY OF MELBOURNE

Evaluated in independent research by staff from the Department of Language, Literacy and Arts Education at the University of Melbourne.

Julie Haydon

Contents

ANTARCTICA

Antarctica is the fifth-largest continent on Earth. It is also the coldest, windiest, driest and highest continent. It is an ice-covered place where no large plants grow, and no land mammals, reptiles or amphibians live.

Antarctica covers an area of more than 13.6 million square kilometres. It is nearly twice the size of Australia, or one-and-a-half times the size of the United States of America.

an Antarctic research base

Antarctica does not belong to one country, and it has no government. People visit Antarctica – usually as tourists, or to do scientific research – but no one lives there all the time.

Chapter 2

DISCOVERING ANTARCTICA

Antarctica was the last continent to be discovered. It is not certain who first saw Antarctica, but sailors began to map Antarctica's coast from their ships in the 1800s. The first confirmed landing was in the mid-1890s.

Over the next few years, several men tried but failed to reach the South Pole, which is the Earth's southernmost point.

a map of Antarctica from the mid 1800s

Finally, a team led by Norwegian Roald Amundsen reached the South Pole in 1911. By then, countries around the world were becoming more and more interested in the frozen continent, and soon seven nations: Argentina, Australia, Chile, France, New Zealand, Norway and the United Kingdom, had laid claim to parts of Antarctica.

Roald Amundsen and his dogs at the South Pole

Talk of a Treaty

As so many nations had made a claim to territory in Antarctica, it was clear that fighting might break out. **Diplomats** from different countries wanted to stop a war from starting, so they began talking about a treaty for Antarctica. A treaty is a written agreement signed by two or more nations.

Explorer Douglas Mawson claims a part of Antarctica for the Commonwealth.

Several countries had already set up research stations in Antarctica where scientists could live and work. Most scientists worked during the summer months when it was not as cold as in winter. Scientists hoped a treaty would allow them to continue their work and to exchange information with scientists from other countries.

Chapter 3

THE ANTARCTIC TREATY

In 1959, 12 nations signed the Antarctic Treaty. The nations were Argentina, Australia, Belgium, Chile, France, Japan, New Zealand, Norway, South Africa, the Soviet Union, the United Kingdom and the United States of America. The Treaty came into force in 1961.

Aims of the Treaty

One of the aims of the Antarctic Treaty was to put on hold all claims to territory in Antarctica. So, although no nation gave up its claim to territory in Antarctica, the nations agreed not to take any further action. Instead, people from the Treaty nations would co-exist peacefully while in Antarctica.

A scientist studies Antarctic weather, using a weather balloon.

Another aim was to promote scientific research and international scientific cooperation. The Treaty nations agreed that it was in the interest of all humans that scientific research in Antarctica continue and that scientists from different countries help each other.

Still another aim was to protect the Antarctic environment, including Antarctica's plants and animals.

In the Antarctic Treaty, the nations agreed that:

- Antarctica shall be used for peaceful purposes only
- freedom of scientific research in Antarctica shall continue
- scientific information and personnel shall be exchanged between countries

- nuclear explosions and the dumping of radioactive waste is not allowed in Antarctica
- inspections of any nation's stations, equipment, supply ships, aeroplanes and helicopters are allowed
- there shall be freedom of access to all areas of Antarctica.

Over the next 20 years, other agreements were created that supported the Antarctic Treaty. These agreements went into more detail about the **conservation** of Antarctica's animals and plants.

The Treaty has been a huge success. There has never been a war in Antarctica, nations cooperate while doing important scientific research, and there are rules in place to protect Antarctica's environment. Today, 46 countries have signed the Antarctic Treaty.

The countries that have signed the Antarctic Treaty are:

Argentina
Australia
Austria
Belarus
Belgium
Brazil
Bulgaria
Canada
Chile
China
Colombia
Cuba
Czech Republic
Democratic People's Republic of Korea
Denmark
Ecuador
Estonia
Finland
France
Germany
Greece
Guatemala
Hungary
India
Italy
Japan
Netherlands
New Zealand
Norway
Papua New Guinea
Peru
Poland
Republic of Korea
Romania
Russian Federation
Slovak Republic
South Africa
Spain
Sweden
Switzerland
Turkey
Ukraine
United Kingdom
United States of America
Uruguay
Venezuela

THE MADRID PROTOCOL

An important issue that was discussed by the Treaty nations in the 1980s was whether mining should be allowed to take place in Antarctica. Some countries thought that it may be possible to mine valuable minerals in Antarctica while still protecting the Antarctic environment. However, some countries did not want any mining to take place. This led to talks about better ways of protecting the Antarctic environment.

In 1991, the Antarctic Treaty nations signed an agreement called the Madrid Protocol. A protocol is a document that is added to a treaty and that includes information to do with the treaty. The Protocol came into force in 1998, and called Antarctica a natural reserve, devoted to peace and science. It set strict rules to protect the Antarctic environment.

Treaty members meet in Madrid in 2003

The Madrid Protocol:

- banned mining in Antarctica
- set strict rules for waste storage and disposal
- banned bringing non-native species of plants and animals into Antarctica without a permit
- set rules to help reduce marine pollution
- said that nations must make plans to prevent and deal with an environmental emergency.

Chapter 5

LIVING IN ANTARCTICA

There are now more than 40 research stations in Antarctica, run by many nations. The people who live and work at the stations must live by the rules set out in the Antarctic Treaty and the Madrid Protocol.

Polish research station on King George Island, Antarctica

It is not only scientists who work in Antarctica. Engineers, mechanics, carpenters, plumbers, electricians, doctors, chefs and station leaders also work at the stations. There are no shops in Antarctica, so everything people need to live and work there must be brought in, usually on large ships.

Scientists in Antarctica

Scientists go to Antarctica to study many different areas of science. Biologists study Antarctica's animals, while botanists study Antarctica's plants. Meteorologists study the atmosphere and weather, glaciologists study Antarctica's ice, and geologists study the Earth's crust in Antarctica and beneath the Southern Ocean.

A scientist tags a Weddell seal.

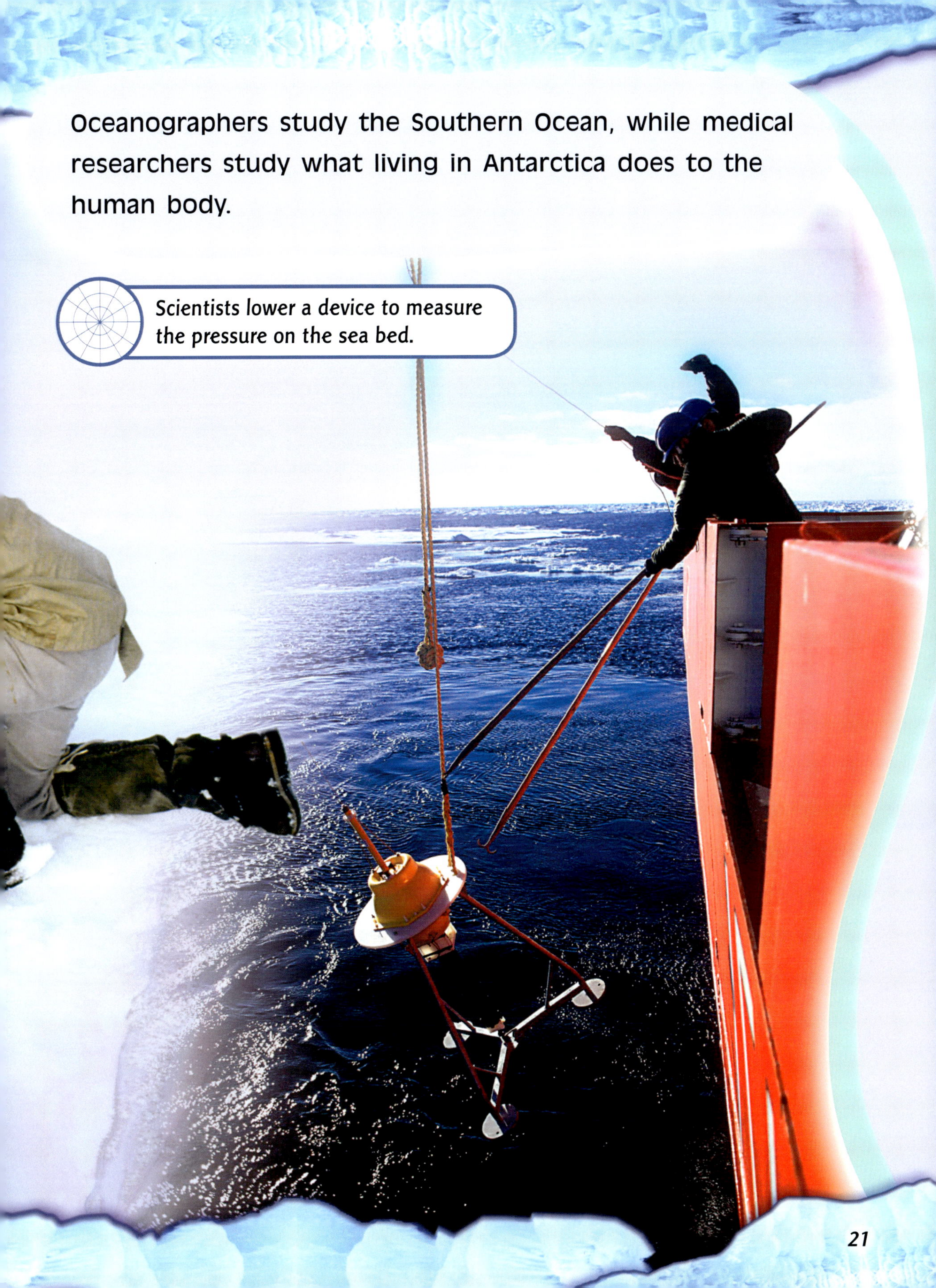

Oceanographers study the Southern Ocean, while medical researchers study what living in Antarctica does to the human body.

Scientists lower a device to measure the pressure on the sea bed.

Chapter 6

TOURISTS IN ANTARCTICA

A small number of tourists visit Antarctica each year. Most arrive on ships that are owned by tour companies. Tourists must also obey the rules set out in the Antarctic Treaty and the Madrid Protocol.

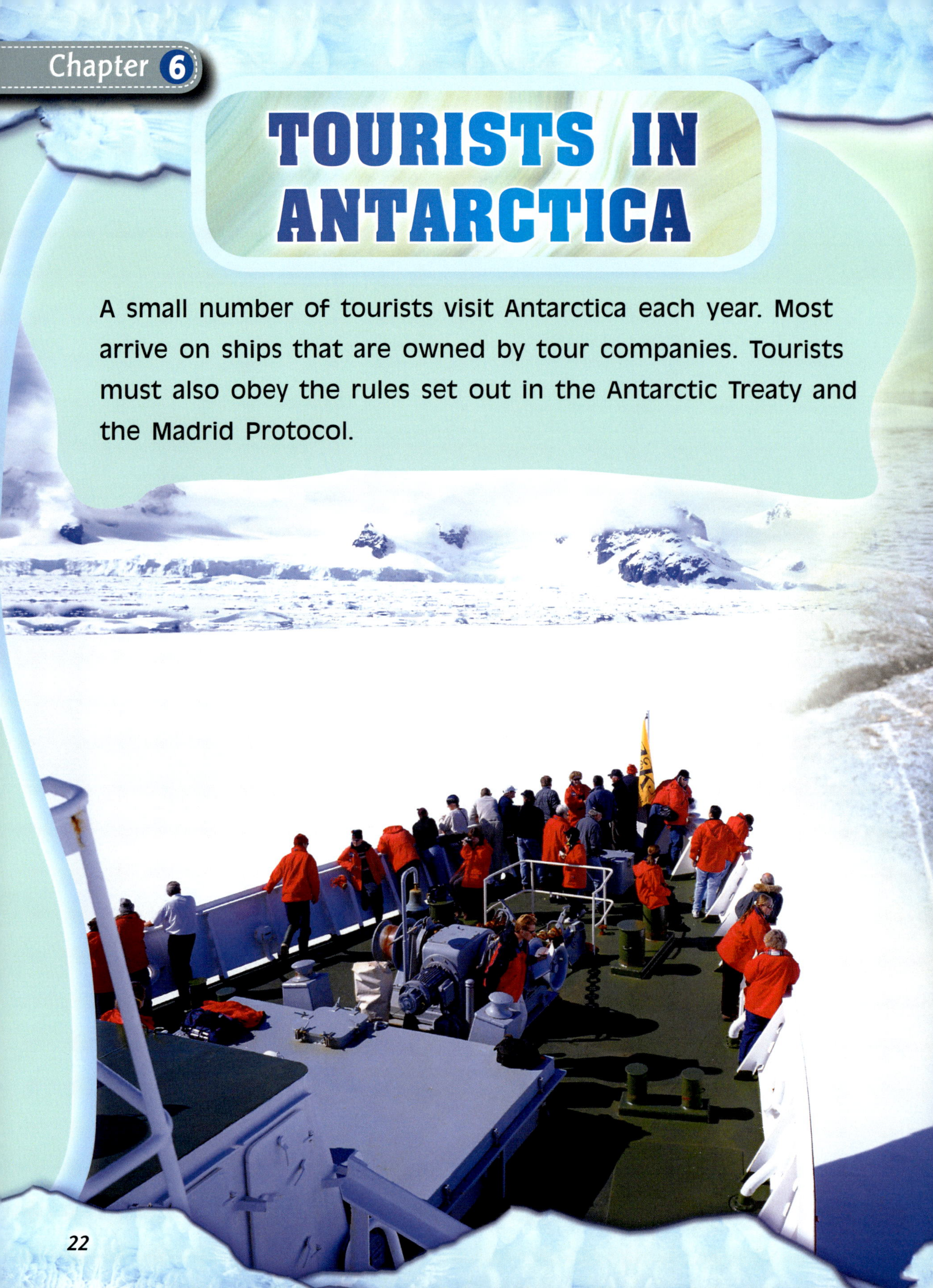

For example, tourists must not leave rubbish or disturb animals or plants. They must obey safety rules and get permits to visit protected areas, and they must not disturb scientific research.

Glossary

conservation protection of the environment and the creatures that live within it

diplomats people appointed to represent a government in its dealings with other countries

Index